JN042728

大学入試

英語長文 plus プラス

頻出テーマ 10

トレーニング問題集

背景知識　　キーワード

宮下卓也 著

旺文社

大学入試

英語長文 *plus*
プラス

頻出テーマ 10

トレーニング問題集

背景知識  キーワード

宮下卓也 著

旺文社

問題編　目次

頻出テーマを学習するメリット

入試英語長文には頻出のジャンルがある

　全国の大学入試問題における出題ジャンルを分析すると，「よく出る」頻出のジャンルが見えてきます。本書では，まず近年の出題歴から頻出のジャンルを割り出しました。すると，ここ10年の傾向として，下のグラフに見られるように「文化」「日常生活」からの出題が特に多いこと，「自然」「社会」「科学・技術」「産業」といったジャンルからも一定の割合で出題されていることがわかりました。また，出題ジャンルにおいては，全般的な傾向(図1)と私大上位レベルの傾向(図2)が類似していることもわかりました。

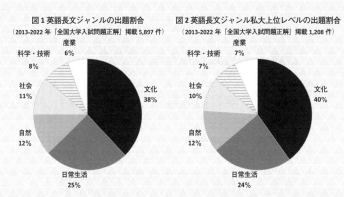

図1 英語長文ジャンルの出題割合
（2013-2022年『全国大学入試問題正解』掲載 5,897件）

科学・技術 8%
産業 6%
社会 11%
自然 12%
日常生活 25%
文化 38%

図2 英語長文ジャンル私大上位レベルの出題割合
（2013-2022年『全国大学入試問題正解』掲載 1,208件）

科学・技術 7%
産業 7%
社会 10%
自然 12%
日常生活 24%
文化 40%

元データ：旺文社『全国大学入試問題正解英語　国公立大編』『私立大編』『追加掲載編』掲載の2013-2022年長文問題(センター試験，共通テスト除く) 5,897件。／私大上位：獨協大，青山学院大，学習院大，北里大，東京理科大，芝浦工業大，成蹊大，成城大，中央大，津田塾大，日本女子大，法政大，明治大，明治学院大，立教大，南山大，同志社大，立命館大，関西大，関西外国語大，関西学院大，西南学院大

私大上位 GMARCH レベルの頻出テーマ

　本書では，先に挙げたジャンルをさらに細かく分析し，2013-2022 年私大上位で頻出の出題テーマの中から，10 題を選び出しました。この頻出テーマは，「出題頻度」はもちろんのこと，「大学入試において知っておくと有利な知識が含まれているかどうか」という観点から絞り込んだものです。例えば，「動物・植物」のテーマでは「先天と後天」の対比についての文章を取り上げましたが，これは人間を含む動物の行動が先天的か後天的かを論じる文章が非常に多く出題されており，そのような文章がどのような流れで書かれているのかということや，類似の文章によくあるキーワードを知っておくことで，入試で有利になると判断したためです。

　また社会問題については，社会問題Ⅰ，Ⅱという形で 2 題取り上げていますが，これは社会問題というテーマが多岐にわたるものであるため，従来からの伝統的な問題と，比較的最近の問題の両方をカバーできるようにと考えたためです。

頻出テーマの学習と長文読解の関係とは？
⇒英文を読むスピードが速くなる！
⇒英文の理解が深まる！

　大学入試問題には，頻出のテーマがあることをわかってもらえたかと思います。それでは，頻出のテーマを学ぶことによって，どのようなメリットがあるのでしょうか。

　メリットの 1 つは，「英文を読むスピードが速くなる」ということです。近年の GMARCH レベルの私大入試問題では，限られた時間の中で大量の英文を読み，問題を解き切ることが求められます。そのような中，頻出のテーマについての知識や理解があれば，「このキーワードは見たことがある」「このような話の流れになるはずだ」などと考えながら読むことができるため，類似の英文を初めて読む場合と比べて，読むスピードを格段にアップさせることができるのです。

　「英文の理解が深まる」こともまた，メリットと言えるでしょう。本書では，設問の解説とは別に，それぞれの頻出テーマについて，テーマに関連する「背景知識」と「キーワード」を載せています。背景知識や厳選したキーワードを押さえておくことは，各テーマについての知識や理解を深め，類似の問題が出題されたときの対応力強化につながります。

背景知識 は長文読解にどう役立つか

　「背景知識」を学ぶメリットについて，もう少し詳しく見ておきましょう。それは，何と言っても，「英文を速く読める」「文章の理解が深まる」「設問が解きやすくなる」ということです。

　例えば，「先天と後天」がテーマの英文があるとします。このとき，英文自体は，ある行動などが「先天的なものか後天的なものか」という対比の流れになるのが一般的ですが，文章だけでなく設問もまた，その対比を前提に作られていることが多いのです。

　このように，各テーマについての「背景知識」があらかじめ頭の中にある程度あれば，英文の展開が予測しやすくなり，英文自体を速く読めるようになるほか，設問も格段に解きやすくなるのです。

キーワード は長文読解にどう役立つか

　それでは，頻出テーマに関連する「キーワード」を知っておくメリットについても，詳しく見ておきましょう。こちらも，メリットは「英文を速く読める」「英文の理解が深まる」「設問が解きやすくなる」ということです。

　例えば，environment「環境」という単語を考えてみましょう。この単語は，環境問題をテーマにした英文でも用いられる単語ですが，「先天と後天」がテーマになっている英文でも頻出のキーワードです。つまり，先天的なことを表すinborn「生まれつきの」などと対比的に，後天的なことを表すのに使われる単語でもあるのです。

　このように，各頻出テーマには，それぞれの英文でよく使われる「キーワード」があります。こういった「キーワード」についての知識を身に付けておくことで，素早く正確に英文を読むことができるようになりますから，設問も非常に解きやすくなるはずです。

問題の取り組み方・英文の読み方のアドバイス

　本書は「頻出テーマ」についての本です。本書を利用して「頻出テーマ」についての理解を深めるため，以下のような手順を参考にして学習しましょう。

　まずは，記載している目標時間内に解き切ることを目指して，問題を解いてみてください。最初は目標時間内に解き切れなくても，気にする必要はありません。ただし，どれくらいの時間がかかったのかを計っておくことは大切です。そうすることで，本書をひととおり学習したあとでもう一度問題を解いたとき，どれくらい時間を短縮できたかがわかります。つまり，どれくらい「頻出テーマ」についての知識や理解が深まったかがわかるのです。

　問題に取り組んだあとは，「問題英文と全文訳」や「設問解説」，「背景知識とキーワード」を使って復習します。その際は，「背景知識とキーワード」のページを先に読み，その内容を「問題英文と全文訳」や「設問解説」のページで確認していくのが効果的です。「問題英文」を再掲しているページでは，テーマに関連するキーワードが青字で示されていますから，色が付いた「キーワード」を意識しながら，「背景知識」を確認するつもりで読み進めましょう。

　本書全体を繰り返し読むことで，「頻出テーマ」についての理解を深めましょう。そうすることで，関連するテーマが大学入試で出題されたときにも，素早く正確に問題を解くことができるはずです。

→では，学習をはじめましょう。

次の英文を読み，設問に答えなさい。

When a light goes out in your room, you ask, "How did that happen?" You might check to see if the lamp is plugged in or if the bulb is burned out, or you might look at homes in your neighborhood to see if there has been a power outage. When you think and act like this, you are searching for *cause-and-effect* relationships — trying to find out what events cause what results. This type of thinking is rational thinking, applied to the physical world. It is basic to science.

Today, we use rational thinking so much that it's hard to imagine other ways of interpreting our experiences. But it wasn't always this way. In other times and places, people relied heavily on superstition* and magic to interpret the world around them. They were unable to analyze the physical world in terms of physical causes and effects.

The ancient Greeks used logic and rational thought in a systematic way to investigate the world around them and make many scientific discoveries. They learned that Earth is round and determined its circumference*. They discovered why things float and suggested that the apparent motion of the stars throughout the night is due to the rotation of Earth. The ancient Greeks founded the science of botany — the systematic study and classification of plants — and even proposed an early version of the principle of natural selection. Such scientific breakthroughs, when applied as technology, greatly enhanced the quality of life in ancient Greece. For example, engineers applied principles articulated by Archimedes and others to construct an elaborate public waterworks, which brought fresh water into the towns and carried sewage away in a sanitary* manner.

When the Romans conquered ancient Greece, they adopted much of Greek culture, including the scientific mode of inquiry, and spread it throughout the Roman Empire. When the Roman Empire fell in the 5th century AD, advancements in science came to a halt in Europe. Nomadic tribes destroyed much in their paths as they conquered Europe and brought in the Dark Ages. While religion held sway in Europe, science continued to advance in other parts of the world.

The Chinese and Polynesians were charting the stars and the planets. Arab nations developed mathematics and learned to make glass, paper, metals, and certain chemicals. Finally, during the 10th through 12th centuries, Islamic people brought the spirit of scientific inquiry back into Europe when they entered Spain. Then universities sprang up. When the printing press was invented by Johannes Gutenberg in the 15th century, science made a great leap forward. People were able to communicate easily with one another across great distances. The printing press did much to advance scientific thought, just as computers and the Internet are doing today.

Up until the 16th century, most people thought Earth was the center of the universe. They thought that the Sun circled the stationary Earth. This thinking was challenged when the Polish astronomer Nicolaus Copernicus quietly published a book proposing that the Sun is stationary, and Earth revolves around it. These ideas conflicted with the powerful institution of the Church and were banned for 200 years.

Modern science began in the 17th century, when the Italian physicist Galileo Galilei revived the Copernican view. Galileo used experiments, rather than speculation, to study nature's behavior. Galileo was arrested for popularizing the Copernican theory and for his other contributions to scientific thought. But, a century later, his ideas and those of Copernicus were accepted by most educated people.

Scientific discoveries are often opposed, especially if they conflict with what people want to believe. In the early 1800s, geologists were condemned because their findings differed from religious accounts of creation. Later in the same century, geology was accepted, but theories of evolution were condemned. Every age has had its intellectual rebels who have been persecuted, condemned, or suppressed but then later regarded as harmless and even essential to the advancement of civilization and the elevation of the human condition.

*superstition「迷信」 circumference「円周」 sanitary「衛生的な」

→次ページへ続きます。

設問　本文の内容と一致するように，次の英文 **(1)**～**(5)** の空所に入る最も適当なものを **(a)**～**(d)** よりそれぞれ 1 つ選び，その記号をマークしなさい。

(1)　According to paragraphs 1 and 2, _____.

- **(a)** people in other times and places did not try to explain the world
- **(b)** when you go out of your room, you should turn off your light
- **(c)** you are using rational thinking when you check to see if neighborhood lights are also out
- **(d)** an example of superstition is when you look to see if your light is on after a power outage

(2)　According to paragraph 3, _____.

- **(a)** botany is the study of the stars, plants and floating things
- **(b)** the ancient Greeks believed that our rotating planet explained why stars moved across the night skies
- **(c)** an elaborately clean system allowed sewage into town while taking clean water out
- **(d)** scientific breakthroughs hardly benefitted people in ancient Greece

(3)　According to paragraphs 4 and 5, _____.

- **(a)** the Greeks adopted Roman culture after conquering them
- **(b)** scientific advancement continued to spread across Europe when nomadic tribes conquered Europe
- **(c)** the Dark Ages destroyed advances in science across the globe
- **(d)** what Gutenberg's invention did for Europe in the 1400s is equivalent to what computer networks do for us today

(4)　According to paragraphs 6 and 7, _____.

(a) Copernicus suggested that Earth was orbited by the Sun

(b) the Church's 16th century beliefs were banned for 200 years

(c) Galileo was arrested for popularizing the theory that the Sun circled Earth

(d) a majority of educated people eventually concluded that Copernicus was correct

(5)　According to paragraph 8, _____.

(a) what we condemn as harmful, we might celebrate later as a breakthrough

(b) religious ideas of creation strongly supported the findings of early geologists

(c) you can be an intellectual rebel at any age because as you grow older you will be harmless

(d) what people believe conflicts with what they want to believe

次の英文を読み，設問に対する最も適切な答えを(**a**)〜(**d**)の中から1つ選びなさい。

"My father used to say, 'Don't raise your voice; *improve your argument!*'"

Nobel Peace Prize winner Desmond Tutu spoke these words during a lecture he gave in Johannesburg in 2004, emphasizing the importance of an active approach to debate and discussion. In particular, Tutu pointed out how the debate and discussion that had characterized the struggle for equality during apartheid* in South Africa seemed to have disappeared. After apartheid, once they had risen to power, Black South Africans tended to expect everyone to agree with their opinions absolutely, with discussion neither expected nor allowed. Tutu thought this was completely the wrong way to present a viewpoint. Instead of just telling people what is right or good, he suggested, those in power must engage the people in public debate in order to create understanding and gain agreement.

This idea of convincing people through logical argument rather than through power is relevant at university as well. In seminar courses especially, students are encouraged to actively participate in debate and discussion, not only among themselves but also with the teacher. One goal of this "active learning" is to provide students with opportunities to think about and talk about course material. Instead of being told what to think, students shape their own thinking through discussion in which opinions are respectfully challenged and debated. Students are encouraged to work with people. Furthermore, it is hoped that through this process students improve their logical and critical thinking skills. One additional benefit of students having to explain their thinking in detail is that teachers can better assess student learning. Even traditional lecture-style classes can benefit from the addition of active learning.

But there are some negative aspects to active learning. It can be very time consuming, especially when discussions go off topic, and there is no guarantee that learning goals will actually be achieved. There is also a risk that students might develop misunderstandings about the course material they are supposed to be studying. Despite these problems, when practiced effectively, active learning increases student participation, which can, in turn, increase student motivation. Students are far more likely to learn — taking in more new information and retaining it for much longer — if they are personally motivated to learn, rather than just wanting to pass the class. Consequently, teachers must plan well in order to find the best ways to personally motivate their students. In short, for active learning to be successful, students will need careful encouragement and guidance from the teacher on how to engage in debate and discussion.

No two students are alike, and no two sets of classes are alike. Therefore, teachers must make adjustments regularly to create learning environments that promote effective active learning. If teachers want students to improve their arguments, then teachers need to give students the best opportunities to practice shaping those arguments and challenging the arguments of others. Active learning provides such environments.

*apartheid「アパルトヘイト」

問 1　What is the main point of the passage?

(a) Active learning helps students improve their argumentative skills.

(b) Active learning helps students understand the instructions of their teacher.

(c) Active learning is difficult to use in university classes.

(d) Active learning prevents students from raising their voices.

問 2　The purpose of the passage is to _____.

(a) convince teachers that students need personal motivation

(b) discuss South African education

(c) explain active learning and how it is used in classes

(d) teach students how to argue powerfully in every class

→次ページへ続きます。

問 3 What can we infer from the passage?

(a) Active learning originated in South Africa.

(b) Desmond Tutu used active learning in lectures.

(c) The writer does not teach seminar and lecture-style classes.

(d) The writer supports the use of active learning in classes.

問 4 According to the passage, which of the following is NOT a benefit of active learning?

(a) Highly motivated students do not need additional guidance.

(b) Students learn how to challenge the opinions of others.

(c) Teachers can better determine students' understanding of course materials.

(d) The thinking of students becomes more logical and critical.

問 5 One of the problems with active learning is that _____.

(a) classes are never the same

(b) discussions sometimes take up more time than planned

(c) students need to learn how to engage in discussion with others

(d) there is a struggle for equality

次の英文を読み，設問に対する最も適切な答えを（a）〜（c）の中から１つ選びなさい。

Strange as it may seem, there is no generally agreed-upon way to distinguish between a "language" and a "dialect." The two words are not objective terms, even among linguists. People often use the terms to mean different things. As used by many people, "language" is what "we" speak and "dialect" is the linguistic variety spoken by someone else, usually someone thought of as inferior. There is no linguistically objective difference between the two. In other contexts, "language" can mean the generally accepted "standard" or government and radio-broadcast language of a country, while "dialects" are versions that are used at home and vary from region to region.

Language varieties tend to be labeled "dialects" rather than "languages" for non-linguistic reasons, usually political or ideological. Often they are not written, or they are spoken by people who are not involved in government. They are generally regarded as being not as "good" as the standard language and consequently have little prestige. In short, the distinction is subjective. It depends on who you are and the perspective from which you judge the varieties.

From a linguistic perspective, no dialect is inherently better than another, and thus no dialect is more deserving of the title "language" than any other dialect. A language can be seen as a group of related dialects. For example, the dominant position of the Parisian dialect in France is largely an accident of history. When the Count of Paris was elected king of France in the tenth century, the language of his court became the "standard" French language. Other related varieties were disdained, as were unrelated varieties, such as Basque in the southwest and Breton in the north. If things had gone differently, the dialect of another French city, such as Marseille or Dijon, might have become the national language of France.

Dialects can be *socially* determined, as Eliza Doolittle learned in *My Fair Lady*. In this play and film, an arrogant language professor claims that he can take a lower-class woman and make her presentable in high society. He succeeds, primarily by changing her speech.

Dialects can also be *politically* determined. The linguist Max Weinreich is often quoted as saying, "A language is a dialect with an army and a navy." His point was that politics often decides what will be called a "dialect" and what will be called a "language." Powerful or historically significant groups have "languages;" their smaller or weaker counterparts have "dialects."

Sometimes what are languages and what are dialects can be *arbitrarily* determined by a person or a government — typically a person or organization endowed with the power to do so. In southern Africa, an early twentieth-century missionary created a language now known as "Tsonga" by declaring three separate languages to be dialects of a single tongue. Conversely, the government of South Africa created two languages by arbitrary declaration — Zulu and Xhosa — even though there is no clear linguistic boundary between them. In many parts of the world, dialects form what is called a "dialect continuum," where no two adjacent dialects are wildly different, but at the ends of the continuum the dialects are mutually unintelligible — speakers of one cannot understand speakers of the other.

Dialect differences are often relatively minor — sometimes just a matter of pronunciation or slight differences in vocabulary (Americans say "elevator" and "cookie;" the British say "lift" and "biscuit"). However, dialect differences are crucial to understanding George Bernard Shaw's famous joke that America and Britain are "two countries separated by a common language." But dialects can also differ so greatly from one another that they are mutually incomprehensible. German speakers from Cologne and German speakers from rural Bavaria can barely understand one another, if at all. Although the Swiss speak German as one of their national languages, few Germans can understand them when they speak their local dialects.

Thus, one of the tests people use to differentiate "language" from "dialect" is mutual intelligibility. In other words, many would say that people speak the same language, meaning dialects of the same language, if they understand each other without too much difficulty. If they don't understand one another, they are considered to be speaking different languages. That seems like a good rule. So why are Cologne German and

Bavarian German, which are not mutually intelligible, not considered separate languages? Or why are Swedish and Norwegian considered separate languages, when Swedes and Norwegians have no trouble understanding one another?

Such questions become even more difficult when speakers of one dialect just don't want to understand speakers of another. One or both groups insist that they speak separate tongues, even though — judging by objective linguistic criteria — they are speaking mutually intelligible dialects of the same language.

It is easy to conclude from all this that the terms "dialect" and "language" have both political and social implications. You might want to ask yourself whether you speak a language or a dialect. It's a trick question, of course, because ultimately, all languages are dialects. You speak both at the same time.

問1　The distinction between a "language" and a "dialect" is

（a）　already agreed upon by most specialists in language.

（b）　difficult to make because they are rather subjective terms.

（c）　not clear until a government makes an official decision.

問2　According to the author of the passage, dialects are called "dialects"

（a）　because linguists decided to give them that name.

（b）　since they are linguistically inferior to "languages."

（c）　for a variety of social and other arbitrary reasons.

問3　A dialect can become a language when a group of people speaking the dialect

（a）　becomes politically dominant.

（b）　improves its speech norms.

（c）　asks the government to make it one.

問 4 George Bernard Shaw's joke is cited

   (a) to point out that what the British call a "biscuit" Americans call a "cookie."

   (b) to emphasize that there are differences between British and American English.

   (c) to stress that America gained its independence from Britain a long time ago.

問 5 According to the author, there are some cases where groups of people who speak mutually intelligible varieties of language

   (a) refuse to accept them as the same language.

   (b) naturally become on good terms with each other.

   (c) do not realize this is true and live separately.

問 6 The case of Cologne German and Bavarian German is cited to show that

   (a) the test people use for differentiating a dialect from a language based on mutual understanding works well.

   (b) their differences are so remarkable that some people think they should be regarded as different languages.

   (c) the task of differentiating a dialect from a language is much more complicated than it appears to be.

問 7 According to the author of this passage,

   (a) to determine what is a "dialect" or a "language" is not solely a linguistic matter.

   (b) what a "language" or a "dialect" is can usually be determined by language users.

   (c) to define a "dialect" or a "language" is a task for linguists, but not for speakers.

次の英文を読み，設問に答えなさい。

　The large white fridge sits on the pavement in Galdakao, a small city on the outskirts of Bilbao, Spain. A wooden fence has been built around it, in the hope of conveying the idea that this is not an abandoned appliance, but a pioneering project aimed at tackling food waste.

　For the past seven weeks, Galdakao, population 29,000, has been home to Spain's first "solidarity fridge," in which residents and restaurants can drop off leftover or unused food otherwise destined for the bin*. Anything left in the fridge can be picked up by anyone who wants it. "I would guess we've saved between 200 and 300 kg from the rubbish bin," said organizer Álvaro Saiz. A typical day might see leftover beans, a few sandwiches and unopened milk cartons left in the fridge.

　The idea came about as Saiz and other members of the city's volunteer association were reflecting on the huge amount of food being thrown out by supermarkets. "We started to think that if even just one of their rubbish bins was (　**1**　) a fridge, people could take advantage of these items." An online search revealed a network of shared fridges in Berlin. He said, "We realized we could do this — so we did."

　It took about a month to work on the paperwork needed for the project, including securing a permit from the city to use public space and obtaining the right legal documents to ensure organizers wouldn't be held liable should anything go wrong with food taken from the fridge. As his group pushed forward with the idea, they heard all sorts of opinions from city residents. Saiz said, "I realized that some people don't support it because they don't understand what we're doing."

　The goal, according to Saiz, isn't to feed people in need. "This isn't charity. It's about making use of food that would otherwise end up in the bin," he said. "It doesn't matter who takes it. (2)At the end of the day it's about recovering the value of food products and fighting against waste."

　There are strict rules for anyone leaving food in the fridge: no raw fish, meat or eggs, packaged or canned goods cannot be past their (3)use-by date and anything prepared at home must include a label detailing when it was made. Volunteers keep an eye on the fridge to throw out anything past its use-by date or homemade dishes that are more than four days old. But that's in theory: so far all food has been taken on a daily basis. All sorts of people have dropped by so far, said Saiz, including those in need who make a special trip to the fridge from nearby towns and a construction worker who took an ice-cream bar — dropped off with just a few days left before its best-before date — during his lunch break.

Last week the city of Murcia, some 400 miles away in the south of Spain, (4) copied the idea and became the second Spanish city to host a solidarity fridge. Saiz has received calls from communities across the country — and from as far as Bolivia — from people interested in setting up similar operations.

The fridge has also allowed local restaurants to stop feeling guilty over their food waste, said Álvaro Llonin of Topa restaurant. "In the past we used to (5) a lot of food — and it was food that was fine to eat." He and the staff at the busy restaurant in the center of Galdakao now regularly make time to drop off their leftovers in the fridge. "You know someone is enjoying it," he said. "It's like giving our food a second chance to end up in someone's stomach."

*bin 「ごみ箱」

問1　上記英文の (1), (5) を埋めるのに最もふさわしい語句をそれぞれ(a), (b), (c), (d)の中から 1 つ選びなさい。

(1)
 (a) bought like　 (b) older than
 (c) replaced with　(d) taken away with

(5)
 (a) drop by　　 (b) remind
 (c) stand by　　(d) throw away

→次ページへ続きます。

問2 上記英文の下線部 (2), (3), (4) に最も近い内容のものをそれぞれ (a), (b), (c), (d) の中から 1 つ選びなさい。

(2) At the end of the day

- (a) After all
- (b) In the afternoon
- (c) The next day
- (d) When all the food is gone

(3) use-by date

- (a) a certain place to keep the food
- (b) a date for the volunteers to buy the food
- (c) a date when the food was made
- (d) a specific date by which the food should be consumed

(4) copied the idea

- (a) collaborated with people in need
- (b) imitated Saiz's food project
- (c) refreshed the mind
- (d) thought about the local environment

問3　上記英文の内容に合致するものを(a)～(i)の中から3つ選びなさい（順不同）。

(a) Galdakao には，賞味期限切れの食品の廃棄を奨励する条例がある。

(b) Galdakao には，未使用の冷蔵庫がたくさん捨てられている。

(c) Galdakao には，人口密度が高いにもかかわらず，街路にごみ箱が少ない。

(d) 生ごみを車の燃料として転用することは，solidarity fridge の活動の一環である。

(e) Saiz は，公共の場所に冷蔵庫を置く許可を得るために数年を費やした。

(f) solidarity fridge から食品を持ち出すとき，人々はお金を払う必要はない。

(g) solidarity fridge はスペイン以外の国でも注目されている。

(h) solidarity fridge は捨てられてしまう食物を有効利用するためのプロジェクトだ。

(i) solidarity fridge の目的は食べ物に困っている人を助けることだ。

次の 2017 年の記事を読み，設問に答えなさい。

More than 10 million UK workers are at high risk of being replaced by robots within 15 years as the automation of routine tasks gathers pace in a new machine age. A report by the consultancy firm Price Waterhouse Coopers (PwC) found that 30% of jobs in Britain were potentially under threat from breakthroughs in artificial intelligence (AI). In some sectors, half the jobs could go. The report predicted that automation would boost productivity and create fresh job opportunities, but it said action was needed to prevent the widening inequality that would result from robots increasingly being used for low-skill tasks.

PwC said 2.25 million jobs were at high risk in wholesale and retailing — the sector that employs most people in the UK — and 1.2 million were at risk in manufacturing, 1.1 million in administrative and support services and 950,000 in transport and storage. The report said the biggest impact would be on workers who had left school at 16 years old or earlier, and that there was an argument for government intervention in (1) education, lifelong learning and job matching to ensure the potential gains from automation were not concentrated in too few hands. Some form of universal basic income might also be considered.

(2) Jon Andrews, the head of technology and investments at PwC, said: "There's no doubt that AI and robotics will rebalance what jobs look like in the future, and that some are more susceptible* than others. What's important is making sure that the potential gains from automation are shared more widely across society and no one gets left behind. Responsible employers need to ensure they encourage flexibility and adaptability in their people so we are all ready for the change. In the future, knowledge will be a commodity so we need to shift our thinking on how we give future generations the necessary skills. Creative and critical thinking will be highly valued, as will emotional intelligence."

Education and health and social care were the sectors seen as least threatened by robots because of the high proportion of tasks seen as hard to automate. Because women tend to work in sectors that require a higher level of education and social skills, PwC said they would be less in jeopardy of losing their jobs than men, who were more likely to work in sectors such as manufacturing and transportation. Thirty-five per cent of male jobs were identified as being at high risk against 26% of female jobs.

The PwC study is the latest to assess the potential for job losses and heightened inequality from AI. Robert Schiller, a Nobel-prize winning US economist, has said the scale of the workplace transformation set to take place in the coming decades should lead to consideration of a "robot tax" to support those machines make redundant. John Hawksworth, PwC's chief economist, said: "A key driver of our industry-level estimates is the fact that manual and routine tasks are more susceptible to automation, while social skills are relatively less automatable. That said, no industry is entirely immune from future advances in robotics and AI.

"Automating more manual and repetitive tasks will eliminate some existing jobs but could also enable some workers to focus on higher value, more rewarding and creative work, removing the monotony from our day jobs. By boosting productivity — a key UK weakness over the past decade — and so generating wealth, advances in robotics and AI should also create additional jobs in less automatable parts of the economy as this extra wealth is spent or invested."

He added that the (3) UK employment rate of just under 75% was at its highest level since modern records began in 1971, suggesting that advances in digital and other labour-saving technologies had been accompanied by job creation. He said it was not clear that the future would be different from the past in terms of how automation would affect overall employment rates.

The fact that it was technically possible to replace a worker with a robot did not mean it was economically attractive to do so and would depend on the relative cost and productivity of machines compared with humans, Hawksworth said. (4) PwC expects this balance to shift in favour of robots as they become cheaper to produce over the coming decades. "In addition, legal and regulatory hurdles will slow down the shift towards AI and robotics even where this becomes technically and economically feasible. And this may not be a bad thing if it gives existing workers and businesses more time to adapt to this brave new world," he said.

*susceptible (adjective) = easily affected, influenced, or harmed by something

→次ページへ続きます。

問 1　Why does the report say that the government should intervene in (1) education?

(a)　to support teachers who are at risk of losing their jobs

(b)　to teach people about universal basic income

(c)　to spread the benefits of the robotic revolution to more people

(d)　to help 16-year olds find employment

問 2　Which of the following from (a) — (e) does NOT match what (2) Jon Andrews said about the future of automation? Choose all the answers that apply.

(a)　Artificial Intelligence will change how the employment market looks in the future.

(b)　Employers will need to think critically about emotional intelligence.

(c)　The training of employees will be necessary to create a flexible workforce.

(d)　Jobs in certain industries are more likely to be lost to robotics than others.

(e)　It will be important to divide the benefits of automation to avoid creating winners and losers.

問 3　Which of the following from (a) — (d) matches what the PwC's chief economist says about the (3) UK employment rate?

(a)　It is high now, but it was higher under the old records before 1970.

(b)　Since 1971, digital technologies have had a negative impact on jobs.

(c)　Less than a quarter of UK workers are unemployed at the moment.

(d)　Even when new technology takes away jobs, other employment opportunities may be made.

問4 Choose the most suitable answer from (a) — (d) which is closest in meaning to the underlined part (4).

(a) Price Waterhouse Coopers believes that cheaper robots of the future will have better balance.

(b) PwC anticipates that it will take many years before workers create cheap robots.

(c) The consultancy firm projects that the cost-performance of automation will continue to improve.

(d) The authors of the report suggest that the relative cost and productivity of robots is most favourable now.

問5 Read sentences (X) and (Y) below and choose the most suitable answer (a) — (d) based on the contents of the passage.

(X) By slowing down the adoption of new technology, regulation can help people adapt to the change caused by robots.

(Y) By investing the profits of automation from an increase in productivity, companies may create other manufacturing jobs.

(a) (X) is correct and (Y) is incorrect.

(b) (X) is incorrect and (Y) is correct.

(c) Both (X) and (Y) are correct.

(d) Neither (X) nor (Y) is correct.

次の英文を読み，設問に答えなさい。

Over the last ten-plus years, we have seen various trends in exercise science. With the arrival of the new year, I thought it would be worthwhile to look back at some of the persistent themes, revelations and surprises from the past decade.

Perhaps most obviously, this has been a decade of greatest HIITs (high-intensity interval trainings), with multiple studies and subsequent media articles asserting that hard but super-short workouts (HIITs) improve fitness and health to about the same extent as much longer, more moderate exercise. Since 2010, I have learned a number of seven-minute, four-minute, one-minute, 20-second and 10-second interval routines, with each workout's declining length increasing its appeal. For many of us, (i) the exercise of choice may be the briefest.

At the same time, though, other studies showed that gentle exercise is also meaningful, even if it barely qualifies as exercise. In one of my favorite studies from this year, researchers found that older women who regularly walked about 3 km a day, or a little more than 4,000 steps, lived longer than women who covered only about 2,000 steps, or 1.5 km. Going those extra kilometers altered how long and well women lived.

In fact, a recurring concern of exercise science over the recent decade has been whether and how exercise affects aging, and the results generally suggest that (ii) it does — and widely so. In various recent studies, active older people's muscles, immune systems, blood cells and even skin appeared biologically younger than those of sedentary* people.

Their brains also tended to look and work differently. In what may be, for me, the most inspiring area of fitness research from the past decade, scientists have found and reaffirmed the extent to which movement, of almost any kind and amount, may remake how we think and feel. In one study after another, physical activity benefitted the brains of children and the middle-aged. It lowered people's risks for dementia* or, if dementia had already begun, slowed memory loss. It also increased brain volume and connections between neurons* and different portions of the brain.

Exercise also seems able to improve moods far more than most of us, including scientists, might have expected a decade ago. In observational studies, physically active people proved to be much less likely to develop depression or anxiety than sedentary people, no matter what types of activities they chose. Walking, jogging, gardening, weight training, swimming, biking, hiking or even rising from an office or living room chair often and walking across the room seemed to make people happier and less vulnerable to mood problems than remaining still. Moreover, in mice, exercise changed the inner workings of some of their neurons in ways that then made them less excitable and less inclined to experience patterns of activity associated with anxiety. Exercise made their cells and brains calmer.

One of the other big themes of exercise science in recent years is that bodies in motion seem to develop interior ecosystems that differ, in fundamental ways, from those of the sedentary. For instance, people who exercise hold different types and amounts of proteins in their bloodstreams, even if they have not been working out recently, and these patterns of proteins may play a role in reducing risks such as diabetes or heart disease.

But many questions remain unanswered regarding the cellular effects of exercise throughout the body. It's also unknown whether changes at the cellular level differ depending on factors like how much and in what fashion we exercise, our age, our health history and whether we happen to be a man, a woman or a mouse. I suspect this will be of great interest to scientists in the decade ahead.

I hope that scientists might eventually help us to better understand why, (iii) with everything we know about the benefits of exercise, so few of us manage to get up and work out regularly. But there could be hope in redirecting our focus. In what may be the most charming fitness study of the 2010s, when sedentary dog owners were told by their veterinarians* that their pets were too heavy and in danger of health problems, they increased both their own and their pets' walking times.

Happy, healthy new year to you, your family and any four-footed workout partners you may have.

*sedentary「座りがちな」 dementia「認知症」 neuron「神経細胞, ニューロン」
veterinarian「獣医」

→次ページへ続きます。

問1　下線部 (i) the exercise of choice の内容に最も近いものを，次の (a)
　　 ～(d) から 1 つ選びなさい。

(a)　our most desirable exercise

(b)　our most necessary exercise

(c)　the routine that allows many choices

(d)　the routine to make a decision

問2　下線部 (ii) it does — and widely so の内容に最も近いものを，次の
　　 (a)～(d) から 1 つ選びなさい。

(a)　a newly invented exercise is effective among various generations

(b)　exercise has a noticeable effect on the way people grow old

(c)　exercise science studies the aging process from a broad
　　　perspective

(d)　this decade is seeing a growing concern with exercise science

問3　下線部 (iii) with everything we know about the benefits of
　　 exercise の内容に最も近いものを，次の (a)～(d) から 1 つ選びなさ
　　 い。

(a)　although we are well aware of the good effects of exercise

(b)　due to our knowledge related to the benefits of exercise

(c)　to prove what we know regarding the good effects of exercise

(d)　because they teach us the benefits of exercise revealed by their
　　　studies

問4　次の (1), (2) の英文について, 正しいものを(a)〜(d)からそれぞれ 1
つずつ選びなさい。

(1)　（Ⅰ）　Doing hard exercise for a brief time is as effective as
doing moderate exercise longer.

（Ⅱ）　Exercise improves mental health, but it should be more
than just walking or moving inside the house.

（a）　（Ⅰ）は本文の内容に合致しているが, （Ⅱ）は合致していない。

（b）　（Ⅰ）は本文の内容に合致していないが, （Ⅱ）は合致している。

（c）　（Ⅰ）も（Ⅱ）も, 本文の内容に合致している。

（d）　（Ⅰ）も（Ⅱ）も, 本文の内容に合致していない。

(2)　（Ⅰ）　Only by continuing to exercise regularly, can we keep a
certain type of protein that reduces the risk of some
diseases.

（Ⅱ）　Veterinarians warn that sedentary people tend to be fat
due to the lack of proper exercise.

（a）　（Ⅰ）は本文の内容に合致しているが, （Ⅱ）は合致していない。

（b）　（Ⅰ）は本文の内容に合致していないが, （Ⅱ）は合致している。

（c）　（Ⅰ）も（Ⅱ）も, 本文の内容に合致している。

（d）　（Ⅰ）も（Ⅱ）も, 本文の内容に合致していない。

6

次の英文を読み，設問に答えなさい。

Friday 15 March, 2019, was a rare day in Venice: On the square in front of the Santa Lucia train station, Venetians outnumbered* tourists. Young Venetians had skipped school to join the global youth climate protest, holding signs with statements such as "If climate was a bank, you'd save it." The movement is especially relevant in Venice, since a 50 cm rise in sea levels could see the city vanish beneath the waves of the lagoon* that surrounds the city.

Important as the climate crisis is, the city faces a more urgent risk: The rising tide of tourists, presently estimated at 25 million a year and expected to reach 38 million by 2025. The tourists now seem to far outnumber the local residents. Europe, already the world's largest tourism market, received 713 million international visitors in 2018, an 8% increase on the previous year, according to the UN World Tourism Organization. While tourism provides significant economic benefit, overtourism* is causing issues including high-priced housing, environmental damage, and the destruction of local life. Issues of overcrowding have brought locals out into the streets to protest. One of the most dramatic was Venice's 2016 *No Grandi Navi* ('No Big Ships') protest, when locals took to the water in small fishing boats to block the passage of six massive cruise ships.

The people of Venice have always looked for ways to protect the equilibrium* of the lagoon and the complex system of commerce around it. In fact, the act of sustaining the lagoon for over a millennium is a singular human achievement because a lagoon by definition is a temporary natural phenomenon. Venice's lagoon would have disappeared in 500 years if it hadn't been for careful environmental protection, sensitive technical solutions, and strict commercial regulation — a historic plan that provides useful lessons for tourism.

A new generation of concerned citizens and businesspeople is taking up that challenge, combining grassroots activism* with socially sensitive, sustainable initiatives to save their island home. Consider waste. What comes into Venice must be removed again via a complex garbage collection system and strict recycling plan. Every day an army of workers knocks on the doors of residents in the city, collecting their carefully separated waste to be shipped away. Unfortunately, the same rules and standards do not apply to tourists — despite the fact that during the peak tourist season the bins around Saint Mark's Square have to be emptied every half an hour.

Troubled by the plastic waste generated by their two hotels, the Romanelli family have taken action, eliminating plastic bottles from their properties, and encouraging guests to use steel drink containers, for which they supply a map showing Venice's historic water fountains. With just 50 rooms and 40 members of staff, they calculate they save 36,000 plastic bottles a year. Multiply that by the estimated 40,000 guest beds in Venice — to say nothing of restaurants or the waste unloaded from cruise ships — and you could save hundreds of millions of plastic bottles a year.

Addressing the issue of waste is just one easily noticeable effort to create a more sustainable tourism in Venice, but there are others. This June will see the launch of 'Fairbnb,' a not-for-profit home-sharing website that tightly controls the number of people who can rent their properties to tourists. Importantly, it will contribute half of its 15% booking fees to social projects in the area. When they book, Fairbnb renters decide which project to support and are invited to visit or participate: In Venice this could mean joining volunteers cleaning graffiti* or helping turn a centuries-old *squero* (boat yard) into an educational centre. Many locals want to bring back the connection between tourists and locals that has been lost. Programmes such as these allow tourists to join locals in their real pursuits, or even just share a drink with them.

This loss of connection between locals and tourists is something that Valeria Duflot and Sebastian Fagarazzi are also concerned with. Through their website, they direct tourists to Venice businesses that support a sustainable local economy — everything from printmakers to photographers to rowers.

Across Europe, other grassroots groups are also fighting to preserve local cultures. Many are arguing that mass tourism causes high rents, pollution, the loss of local shops and the spread of low-wage jobs.

It is this focus on the liveability* of a city that Venetian data scientist Fabio Carrera believes is the key to Venice's future. If a city cannot retain its own population, no amount of tourist tax will be able to prevent its inevitable decline and death. No other city faces a bigger tourism challenge, says Carrera — but given Venice's uniquely contained and complex character, no other place is better prepared to meet the challenge of sustainable tourism. "Younger generations have been out in the world," he says. "They see other possibilities and want to bring that vision back to Venice."

*outnumber「数で上回る」 lagoon「潟湖(砂州やサンゴ礁によって外海から隔てられて湖沼化した地形)」 overtourism「オーバーツーリズム，観光公害」 equilibrium「均衡の取れた状態」 grassroots activism「草の根の市民運動」 graffiti「落書き」 liveability「住みやすさ」

問1 本文の意味，内容にかかわる問い(1)〜(3)それぞれの答えとして，本文にしたがって最も適当なものを(a)〜(d)から1つ選びなさい。

(1) Why didn't some Venetian students attend school one Friday in March, 2019?

(a) Because some school buildings had been damaged by flood

(b) Because they decided to join a demonstration about environmental issues

(c) Because crowds around the main station had made travelling to school impossible

(d) Because they wanted to protest the government's plan to raise the amount of fees that non-local students must pay

(2) What is one reason NOT mentioned to explain what the people of Venice have done in previous centuries to allow the lagoon to survive so long?

(a) The use of technology to help protect it

(b) The careful preservation of its environment

(c) A limit on the number of tourists allowed to visit there

(d) Tight controls over the way people conducted trade there

(**3**)　　What benefit does the writer mention as coming from the use of 'Fairbnb'?

　（**a**）　It provides employment to local people.

　（**b**）　It guarantees tourists the cheapest rates.

　（**c**）　Some of the money tourists spend is donated to the local community.

　（**d**）　The company has a reputation for being environmentally responsible.

問2　次の(**1**)~(**5**)の文の中で，本文の内容と一致するものには(**a**)の記号を，一致しないものには(**b**)の記号を，また本文の内容からだけではどちらとも判断しかねるものには(**c**)の記号を書きなさい。

(**1**)　　The author believes that the problem of climate change needs to be dealt with before the problem of overtourism.

(**2**)　　Fewer cruise ships visited Venice after the *No Grandi Navi* movement protest.

(**3**)　　The author's opinions about the problems Venice faces are based on her experiences living there.

(**4**)　　The map provided by the Romanelli family helps tourists find places to recycle plastic bottles.

(**5**)　　Fabio Carrera believes that the youth of Venice are eager to address the problem of overtourism.

問3　本文の内容を最もよく表しているものを(**a**)~(**e**)から1つ選びなさい。

　（**a**）　The future of eco-tourism

　（**b**）　How climate change is threatening Venice

　（**c**）　The pros and cons of cruise ships to the Venetian economy

　（**d**）　Various strategies to save a city from the effects of excess tourism

　（**e**）　Why the cost of housing in Venice has been affected by the growth in tourist numbers

次の英文を読み，設問に答えなさい。

Most children are taught the (1) virtue of honesty from fairy tales and other stories. The famous story of Pinocchio, who begins life as a puppet*, teaches the importance of telling the truth. Every time Pinocchio lies, his nose grows longer and longer. Another story about the boy who "cried wolf" and then lost all of his sheep illustrates how lying can (2) lead to the loss of trust. In the United States, young children learn the tale of young George Washington, who finally admits to his father that he cut down a cherry tree. These types of stories show children that "honesty is the best policy." Still, if this is the case, then why do so many people lie? The fact is that human beings lie for many reasons.

One reason for lying has to do with minimizing a mistake. While it is true that everyone makes mistakes from time to time, some people do not have the courage to admit their errors because they fear the blame. For example, students might lie to their teachers about unfinished homework. They might say that they left their work at home when, in fact, they did not do the work at all. These students do not want to seem irresponsible*, so they make up an excuse — a lie — to save face.

Another reason people lie is to get out of situations that they do not want to be in or cannot manage. For example, if a company decides to have a weekend meeting, one of the managers might not feel like attending. She may call her boss and give this excuse: "I've been fighting off a cold all week, and I wouldn't want to risk giving it to anybody else. I'll be sure to get all of the notes on Monday." When individuals do not want to tell the truth and face the consequences, they use lies to avoid difficulties.

In contrast, some people might tell a "white lie" when they do not want to hurt someone's feelings. For example, if a good friend shows up with an unattractive new haircut, one could be truthful and say, "That haircut is awful. What were you thinking?!" A more likely scenario is to say, "It's very original! It suits you," and spare the friend's feelings. These types of lies are generally not considered negative or wrong. In fact, many people who have told the truth to those they love, only to see the negative reaction, wish they *had* told a white lie. Therefore, white lies can be useful in (3) maintaining good relationships.

A somewhat different reason for lying has to do with self-protection. Parents, particularly those with small children, may teach their children to use this type of "protective" lie in certain circumstances. What should children do if a stranger calls while the parents are out? Many parents teach their children to explain that mom and dad are too busy to come to the phone at that time. In this situation, protective lying can (**4**) harm or disaster.

People lie for many reasons, both good and bad. However, before you resort to lying in order to cover up mistakes or to avoid unpleasant situations, perhaps the motives for your lies should be carefully examined. Your lies may one day be exposed and cause severe embarrassment or the loss of people's trust.

*puppet「操り人形」 irresponsible < responsible

問 1 下線部 (1), (2), (3) に代わる語句として最も適切なものを選択肢から選びなさい。

(1) virtue
　（ a ） cost　（ b ） spirit　（ c ） value　（ d ） vice

(2) lead to
　（ a ） result from　（ b ） result in　（ c ） run across　（ d ） run into

(3) maintaining
　（ a ） constructing　（ b ） fixing　（ c ） improving　（ d ） preserving

問 2 空所 (**4**) に入る最も適切なものを選択肢から選びなさい。

　（ a ） cause　（ b ） conceal　（ c ） prevent　（ d ） promote

→次ページへ続きます。

問3 第1，2パラグラフの内容と一致するものを選択肢から<u>二つ</u>選びなさい。

(a) The lesson that children take from the stories of Pinocchio and the boy who "cried wolf," as well as the tale of young George Washington, is the importance of being honest.

(b) There would be no lying if people knew that "honesty is the best policy."

(c) One reason for lying is related to trying to make one's mistakes as small or as unimportant as possible.

(d) Only those who lack courage can admit the mistakes they make occasionally.

(e) Students who have not finished their homework confess to their teachers, in order to avoid punishment.

問4 第3，4パラグラフの内容と一致するものを選択肢から<u>二つ</u>選びなさい。

(a) A company manager who does not want to attend a weekend meeting may tell her boss on the phone that she has fully recovered from a cold but needs a few more days of rest.

(b) If you say, "That haircut is awful," to a good friend of yours who appears with a new haircut that you don't find attractive, it means you are telling a white lie.

(c) By telling your friend that their awful haircut suits them, you are telling a white lie to avoid hurting their feelings.

(d) White lies are disapproved of by most people.

(e) Many people regret having told the truth, rather than a white lie, to those they love.

問5　第5，6パラグラフの内容と一致するものを選択肢から一つ選びなさい。

(a) People often lie about how to protect themselves.

(b) Children may be taught to lie in order to protect their parents.

(c) If a person children don't know appears when the parents are not at home, the children should immediately let them know by phone.

(d) When you think you have to lie, it might be better to carefully consider the reasons for doing so.

8

次の英文を読み，設問に答えなさい。

A new study of US twins suggests that genes may help determine how religious a person is, as well as that the effects of a religious upbringing may fade with time.

Until about 25 years ago, scientists assumed that religious behavior was simply the product of a person's socialization — or (1). But more recent studies, including those on adult twins who were raised apart, suggest genes contribute about 40% of the variability in people's belief in religion.

However, it is not clear how that contribution changes with age. A few studies on children and teenagers — with biological or adoptive parents — show that children tend to (2) the religious beliefs and behaviors of the parents with whom they live. This suggests genes play a small role in religiousness at that age.

Now researchers led by Laura Koenig, a graduate student of psychology at the University of Minnesota, have tried to (i) tease apart how the effects of nature and nurture vary with time. Their study suggests that as adolescents grow into adults, genetic factors become more important in determining how religious a person is, while environmental factors wane.

The team gave questionnaires to 169 pairs of identical twins (100% genetically identical) and 104 pairs of fraternal twins (50% genetically identical) born in Minnesota.

The twins — all males, living independently, and in their early 30s — were asked how often they currently went to religious services, prayed, and discussed religious teachings. This was compared with when they were growing up and (3). Then each participant answered the same questions regarding their mother, father, and their twin.

The twins believed that when they were younger, all of their family members — including themselves — shared similar religious behavior. But in adulthood only the identical twins reported maintaining that similarity, while in contrast, (ii) fraternal twins were about a third less similar than they were as children.

"That would suggest genetic factors are becoming more important and growing up together less important," says team member Matt McGue, a psychologist at the University of Minnesota.

Michael McCullough, a psychologist at the University of Miami, agrees. "To a great extent, you can't be who you are when you're living under your parents' roof. But once you leave the nest, you can begin to let your own preferences and dispositions shape your behavior," he told *New Scientist*. "Maybe, ultimately, we all decide what we're most comfortable with, and it may have more to do with our own make-up than how we were treated when we were adolescents," says McGue.

About a dozen studies have shown that religious people tend to share other personality traits, although it is not clear whether they arise from genetic or environmental factors. These include the ability to get along well with others and being conscientious, working hard, being punctual, and controlling one's (**4**).

McGue says the new work suggests that being raised in a religious household may affect a person's long-term psychological state less than previously thought. But he says the influence from this (**5**) may re-emerge later on, when the twins have families of their own. He also points out that the findings may not be universal because the research focused on a single population of US men.

問 1　Fill in each of the blanks (1) through (5) with the most suitable item from (a) to (h).

(a) own impulses　　　　　(b) genetic make-up

(c) mirror　　　　　　　　(d) on their own

(e) living with their families　(f) late-stage parenting

(g) early socialization　　　(h) nurturing

→次ページへ続きます。

問 2 (i) tease apart here means how scientists _____.

(a) unleash new theories to explain complex phenomena

(b) disentangle complex phenomena in order to build plausible explanations

(c) criticize past theoretical explanations and disregard conventional wisdom

(d) create new theories from old ones in order to expand human knowledge

問 3 (ii) fraternal twins were about a third less similar than they were as children means that _____.

(a) fraternal twins will more likely behave in similar ways when they live independently

(b) identical twins will more likely behave in different ways when they live independently

(c) because both identical and fraternal twins share at least 50% of their genetic make-up, they are likely to hold similar beliefs in adulthood

(d) identical twins will more likely behave in similar ways when they live independently because there is less genetic variability

問 4 According to Koenig's study, what is the role of genetics in determining a person's religiousness?

(a) The early effects of a person's genetic make-up slowly fade as they grow into adulthood.

(b) Among those surveyed, the findings indicate that genes caused about 40% of the difference in the degree of religious belief.

(c) We can now predict that 40% of any given population will be religious.

(d) A person's genetic make-up is the key determinant of their religious beliefs.

問 5　Which of the following statements would best summarize the passage?

(a)　Early socialization is more important than one's environment in determining religious behavior.

(b)　Genetics matters more than parenting in determining religious behavior.

(c)　Genetics as well as early socialization is a significant determinant of religiousness.

(d)　Nature, rather than nurturing, is now understood to be a far more robust determinant of religious belief.

9

次の英文を読み，設問に答えなさい。

1　The ways in which people communicate during conflicts vary widely from one culture to another. The kind of rational, straight-talking, calm yet assertive approach that characterizes Euro-American disagreements is not the norm in other cultures. For example, in traditional African-American culture, conflict is characterized by a greater tolerance for expressions of intense emotions than is the rational, calm model taught in mainstream U.S. culture. Ethnicity isn't the only factor that shapes a communicator's preferred conflict style. The degree of assimilation also plays an important role. For example, Latino Americans with strong cultural identities tend to seek compromise more than those with weaker cultural ties.

2　Not surprisingly, people from different regions manage conflict quite differently. In individualistic cultures like that of the United States, the goals, rights, and needs of each person are considered important, and most people would agree that it is an individual's right to stand up for himself or herself. By contrast, collectivist cultures (more common in Latin America and Asia) consider the concerns of the group to be more important than those of any individual. In these cultures, the kind of assertive behavior that might seem perfectly appropriate to a North American would seem rude and insensitive.

3　Another factor that distinguishes the assertiveness that is so valued by North Americans and northern Europeans from other cultures is the difference between high- and low-context cultural styles. Low context cultures like that of the United States place a premium on being direct and literal. By contrast, high-context cultures like that of Japan value self-restraint and avoid confrontation. Communicators in these cultures derive meaning from a variety of unspoken rules, such as the context, social conventions, and hints. Preserving and honoring the face of the other person are prime goals, and communicators go to great lengths to avoid any communication that might risk embarrassing a conversational partner. For this reason, what seems like "beating around the bush" to an American would be polite to a Japanese. In Japan, for example, even a simple request like "close the window" would be too straightforward. A more indirect statement like "it is somewhat cold today" would be more appropriate. Another example is the Japanese reluctance to simply say "no" to a request. A more likely answer would be "Let me think about it for a while," which anyone familiar with Japanese culture would recognize as a refusal. When indirect communication is a cultural norm, it is unreasonable to expect more straightforward approaches to succeed.

4 It isn't necessary to look at Eastern cultures to encounter cultural differences in conflict. The style of some other familiar cultures differs in important ways from the northern European and North American norm. These cultures see verbal disputes as a form of intimacy and even a game. Americans visiting Greece, for example, often think they are witnessing an argument when they are overhearing a friendly conversation. A comparative study of American and Italian nursery school children showed that one of the Italian children's favorite pastimes was a kind of heated debating that Italians called *discussione*, which Americans would regard as arguing. Likewise, research has shown that working-class Jewish speakers of eastern European origin used arguments as a means of being sociable.

5 Within the United States, the ethnic background of communicators also plays a role in their ideas about conflict. When African-American, Mexican-American, and white American college students were asked about their views regarding conflict, some important differences emerged. For example, white Americans seem more willing to accept conflict as a natural part of relationships, whereas Mexican Americans describe the short- and long-term dangers of disagreeing. Whites' willingness to experience conflicts may be part of their individualistic, low-context communication style of speaking directly and avoiding uncertainty. It's not surprising that people from more collective, high-context cultures that emphasize harmony among people with close relationships tend to handle conflicts in less direct ways. With differences like these, it's easy to imagine how two friends, lovers, or fellow workers from different cultural backgrounds might have trouble finding a conflict style that is comfortable for both of them.

10

→次ページへ続きます。

問 1 Choose the best way to complete the following sentences about Paragraphs **1** to **5**.

(1)   In Paragraph **1** the authors mainly describe
(2)   In Paragraph **2** the authors mainly describe
(3)   In Paragraph **3** the authors mainly describe
(4)   In Paragraph **4** the authors mainly describe
(5)   In Paragraph **5** the authors mainly describe

- (a) American people's reluctance to understand Japanese people's indirect communication style.
- (b) how people from different ethnic backgrounds struggle to find a way to handle conflict even when they are from the same country.
- (c) how people's tendencies to communicate directly or indirectly depend on cultural norms.
- (d) that assertiveness is perceived differently between those who value the individual and those who place importance on the group.
- (e) the importance of ethnicity compared with assimilation in communicating during conflicts.
- (f) the inability of Japanese people to say "no."
- (g) the differences in communication styles during conflicts for different cultures.
- (h) the different views toward arguing in different countries and cultural groups.

問 2 Choose the BEST way to complete each of these sentences that does NOT agree with the passage.

(1)   Euro-Americans

- (a) are known for their straight-talking approaches.
- (b) disagree in a calm but assertive way.
- (c) follow the norm of other cultures in their disagreements.
- (d) have less tolerance of expressions of intense emotion than African-Americans.

(2) Japanese people

(a) prefer to make simple requests.

(b) rely on unspoken rules.

(c) try not to embarrass their conversation partners.

(d) usually refuse indirectly.

(3) Arguments

(a) are a part of the culture of Italians from a young age.

(b) are not seen as negative in all cultures.

(c) are often mistaken by Americans visiting Greece as friendly conversations.

(d) are viewed as a game in some cultures.

(4) Conflict

(a) is a natural part of relationships to white Americans.

(b) is considered differently by white Americans and Mexican Americans.

10

(c) is handled less directly in high-context cultures.

(d) is more common in collectivist cultures.

出典一覧

問題1 Hewitt, PG et al, "Conceptual Integrated Science", 1st Ed, ©2007. Reprinted by permission of Pearson Education, Inc.

問題2 明治学院大学

問題3 "What's the Difference between Dialects and Languages?" from *The Five-Minute Linguist*, edited by EM Rickerson and Barry Hilton, 2012. Used by permission of Equinox Publishing Ltd.

問題4 "The solidarity fridge: Spanish town's cool way to cut food waste" by Ashifa Kassam, from *The Guardian*. Used by permission.

問題5 "Millions of UK workers at risk of being replaced by robots, study says" by Larry Elliott, from *The Guardian*. Used by permission.

問題6 "A Decade of Fitness" by Gretchen Reynolds, from *The New York Times*. Used by permission.

問題7 "Sinking city: how Venice is managing Europe's worst tourism crisis" by Paula Hardy, from *The Guardian*. Used by permission.

問題8 "The Truth Behind Lying" from *Great Writing 4: Great Essays* by Keith S Folse, April Muchmore-Vokoun, Elena Vestri Solomon, Cengage Learning Inc. Reproduced by permission. www.cengage.com/permissions

問題9 "Genes contribute to religious inclination" by Maggie Mckee, 16/03/2005. ©2005 New Scientist Ltd. All rights reserved. Distributed by Tribune Content Agency.

問題10 "Understanding human communication" by Ronal Adler, George Rodman. Reproduced with permission of the Licensor through PLSclear.